The
Easiest
Way

by Mabel Katz

Your Business, Press

The Easiest Way

Solve your problems and take the road to love, happiness, wealth and the life of your dreams.

by Mabel Katz

Publisher's Cataloging-in-Publication
Katz, Mabel
The Easiest Way: Solve your problems and take the road to love, happiness, wealth and the life of your dreams | Mabel Katz – Special Edition. pbk. p.cm.

LCCN TX 7-351-138   **ISBN** 978-0-9825910-3-1

1. Self realization   **2.** Control (Psychology)
3. Problem solving I. Title

BF637.S4K38 2004   158.1
BQI04-200061

The Easiest Way Special Edition
Copyright © 2009 Mabel Katz

Cover Photo and Design: Erika Aguilar
Book Design: Eduardo Venegas
Translator: Sol Rapoport
Editor: Mirta J. Atlas

Your Business, Press

PO Box 427
Woodland Hills, CA 91365
(818) 668-2085
support@mabelkatz.com
www.BusinessByYou.com

PRINTED IN THE UNITED STATES OF AMERICA

Dedication

To my dear sons, Lyonel and
Jonathan, who I love with all
my heart. I am so proud of
both of you and I sincerely
hope you discover the easiest
way more quickly than I did.
I wrote this book for you.

Acknowledgements

I wish to express my gratitude to the following:

To God, for his patience, his Love, for being always with me, even when I wasn't aware of it.

To Dr. Ihaleakalá Hew Len, for being my inspiration, my Teacher, my opportunity, for all his lessons, and for putting up with me. This book is a product of all that I have learned from him in the last four years.

To Kamailelauli'I Rafalovich, for the incredible work that she does, for her wisdom, patience and dedication.

To The Foundation of I, Inc., for all the dedication, work and the materials they make available to us.

To Tony Rose, for his positive support and suggestions. When I mentioned the overwhelming response from my radio show and the positive results, he immediately said to me, "You have to write a book." In that very moment I realized how important it was to finish this book.

To Betina Rapoport, for always being there to help me "put my feet on the ground" and rethink and reconsider my ideas and projects.

To Maria Mayer, because she was the first editor with whom I worked on this book who encouraged me by telling me it had been helpful to her to read it.

To Fernando Gomez, for his encouraging words, specially coming from someone with his experience.

To Diana Valori, for her centered thinking and her clarity. She was the only one who could put all the pieces together and finish the puzzle.

To my mother, for giving me the opportunity to come into this world and for always supporting me in all my projects, decisions and the radical changes in my life.

To Mirta J. Atlas and Julio Lublinerman, for their perceptive book recommendations, which brought me amazing growth urges.

To Alejandro Katz, for his love and dedication to the family, which made it possible for me to be where I am.

To Julia Jacobo, for her warmth, love, and dedication to my children and for all her help.

To Cielo Millstein, for all her collaboration and her contributions to the Q & A.

To Ellen Reid, my book shepherd, who, with her expertise helped me every step of the way.

To all of you, who pass or will pass sometime through my life.

Thank you. Thank you very much.

 *Preface*

I grew up knowing I had a big secret. I knew how to get what I wanted, but I also had the "belief" that you had to work hard to get it, that everything came with a price and was terribly expensive.

Later on in life, I had everything one could desire materially and emotionally: a new house, new cars, enough money to travel and buy whatever I wanted, a loving husband, two healthy and beautiful children. Yet I wasn't happy. On the contrary, I was a very angry person.

One day I recognized this anger and resentment in my oldest son Jonathan. Seeing this was such a shock. It really woke me up and I said to myself, "Mabel, you have to do something about it. You cannot go on like this. This has to stop."

In that moment I began my search. The first seminar I attended was on the topic of anger. It was conducted by Dr. Bill, to whom I am immensely grateful for all that I have learned from him. I later practiced yoga and visualization with Anna, which allowed me to get in touch with the incredible power that we have inside to create and attract what we want. I experienced the most radical change when my friend Mirta lent me a metaphysical book. Incredible! That book really woke me up. It talked a lot about Jesus (remember now that I am Jewish), but I felt good reading it. I didn't want to let it go. I would have liked to have read it all in one day. I began to practice the techniques that the author mentioned in the book and they worked. This confirmed once again that the power to change things was inside of me and did not depend on anyone or anything else. I thought, "There's something big here, very big," and my heart started to beat in a different way. I was happier than ever before. I felt an inner happiness that cannot be described with words; it has to be lived, felt, and experienced to be known.

After trying different paths, among them Rebirthing, I found Ho'oponopono, an ancient Hawaiian art that teaches us how to resolve our problems. Thanks to its teachings, I discovered that LIFE CAN BE EASY, certainly much easier than I had imagined. After much searching, I have finally found my way. It is a way that allows me to be at peace in the middle of a tempest; it allows me to feel free independently of what is happening around me or of what others are doing or saying. This is why I have chosen to share in this small book, all I have learned up until now.

I am immensely grateful for this opportunity.

Introduction

My teacher Ihaleakalá once told me a
Hawaiian story of creation that goes like
this: When God created the Earth and put
Adam and Eve here, he told them that this
was paradise and that they didn't have
to worry about anything, that He would
provide them with everything they needed.
He also told them that He would give them
a gift, the opportunity to choose, to make
their own decisions, that He would give
them the gift of **free will**. And so, He created
the apple tree. He told them, "This is called

thinking. You do not need it. I can provide everything for you. You should not worry, but you can choose to stay with me or to take your own path."

I would like to make clear that the problem was not the eating of the apple, the problem was not taking responsibility and saying, "I'm sorry." When God asked, Adam said, "She made me do it." And so this is how Adam had to go in search of his first job. Just like Adam, we are always biting the apple. We always think that we know best. We do not realize that there is another way, that there is an easier way.

In Eckhart Tolle's book, *The Power of Now*, he says, *"The most common ego identifications have to do with possessions, the work you do, social status and recognition, knowledge and education, physical appearance, personal and family history…None of these is you. Do you find this frightening? Or is it a relief to know this? All of these things you will have to relinquish sooner or later…You will know it at the latest when you feel death approaching. Death is a stripping away of all that, that is not you. The secret of life is to 'die before you die' and find that there is no death."* And later on he says, *"The good news is that you can free yourself from your mind."* He refers to this voice that talks to us all the time in our heads, *"The voice comments, speculates, judges, compares, complains, likes, dislikes and so on. The voice isn't necessarily relevant to the situation you find yourself in at the time; it may be reviving the recent or distant past or rehearsing or imagining possible future situations."*

Life is a repetition of memories that are like **chips**, or **tapes** that play in our minds 24 hours a day. They drive us and influence us without us even being aware of them. We cannot avoid them, but we can choose to stop the tapes. In this book I use certain terminology and concepts that I would like to clarify. Many of them are based on **Ho'oponopono**, an ancient Hawaiian art. In the last chapter of this book I describe techniques and tools specific to this art. Ho'oponopono teaches us how to erase the aforementioned tapes, how to eliminate the chips that are of no good for us or that do not work in our lives anymore. It shows us how to lift the fog. Only when we erase and clean these programs can we discover who we really are and the power that we possess. By erasing, cleaning, and removing ancient memories, we allow for these to be transmuted and we start to experience our true Self.

Ho'oponopono is a process of forgiveness, repentance, and transformation. Every time that we use any of its tools, we are taking 100% responsibility and asking for forgiveness (from ourselves). We learn that everything that appears in our lives is only a projection of our "programs." We can choose to let them go and observe them, or to react and get caught up in them.

We all have an eraser incorporated within us, a delete key, but we forget how to use it. Ho'oponopono helps us to remember the power that we have to choose between **erasing** (letting go) or reacting, being happy or suffering. It is only a matter of choice in every moment of our lives. When this book mentions **"cleaning"** or **"erasing"** I am referring to the use of Ho'oponopono's techniques to erase the memories and thoughts that create our problems.

In addition, throughout the book I mention the **Indigo Children**. These are children who have been born in different parts of the planet who know exactly who they are and are very clear on why they are here and what their missions are. They are conscious of the existence of others like them and they communicate telepathically among themselves. They have psychic gifts. They speak to us about real Love. They tell us that we ourselves are Love.

I would also like to clarify that when I use the word God, I am not doing so in a religious context. For me, God is that part of us that knows everything. It can't really be defined, it has no name, it is only an experience. You will also note that I use the word God synonymously with the word Love. I am referring to unconditional Love, the one that can heal everything. This is the Love that has all the answers.

When I mention Jesus' proverbs I am also not doing so in a religious context. The purpose is to remind the reader that we have always had teachers who have tried to wake us up and make us see the truth. For example, Jesus spoke of turning the other cheek, but that is a concept that we are still struggling with today. Nonetheless, when we erase (let go) instead of reacting, we are turning the other cheek, the cheek of Love. Letting go instead of reacting is turning the other cheek.

The aim of this brief summary of basic concepts that I intend to use and transmit, is to clarify my starting point. My hope is that the reader will find in this book a fountain of techniques, tools, and knowledge that will allow him/her to feel, make decisions, and live with the inner freedom, peace, and love that is the inheritance of all human beings.

Chapter I

Who am I?

The only reason for our existence is to discover who we are.

— Dr. Ihaleakalá Hew Len

A professor goes to visit a Zen teacher and upon his arrival says, "Hello, I am Dr. Smith. I am this. I am that. I do this and that, etc., etc. and I would like to learn Buddhism." The teacher responds, "Would you like to sit down?" "Yes." "Would you like a cup of tea?" "Yes." So the teacher pours some tea in the cup and continues to do so even when the cup is full and begins to overflow. The Dr. exclaims, "The cup is overflowing! And the tea is spilling out!" To this the teacher responds, "Exactly. You have come with your cup full, and it is overflowing. In this manner, how can I give you anything? You are already flooded with all of that knowledge. If you do not come to me empty and open I cannot give you anything..."

I have lived the major part of my life thinking that I was Mabel, Argentine, Jewish, wife, mother, accountant, etc., etc. I defined myself through my titles, and my roles. I had my cup full with knowledge that was distancing me from myself. I only believed in that which I could touch or see. For me, all those who spoke of the esoteric were "crazies" or "bohemians" that had no idea what they were saying and did not belong to this world. This way of thinking brought me much suffering. However, when I discovered that I was much more than just my physical body, a new world of infinite possibilities opened up for me, a world without bars. When I realized the power that my thoughts had, I understood the why and how of life.

Many of us live with these bars. We feel them, but we do not see them because they are invisible. These bars are our beliefs, our judgments and opinions, and most of all what we think of ourselves. In the precise instant that we decide to become conscious of who we are, these bars open up, and we realize that we are free and that we have always been. In this way we are able to escape the prison that we ourselves have created.

We were told that we are human beings and we decided to believe it. If we think we are defenseless beings without any power, that is what we are going to manifest in our lives. We are kings of our own kingdom and we can build and manifest all that we can imagine. It is all up to us.

We are all children of God and we all have been created in His image. We are creators. How do we create? With our thoughts. It's that simple.

In the introduction of this book I speak of the Indigo Children. Many of the messages from these children arrive through James Twyman, who communicates with them the majority of the time through telepathy. They speak to us about the necessity of "pretending," and they tell us, "Pretend that you are enlightened. Pretend that you are loved by God. Pretend that you are perfect just the way you are. Take a deep breath now and PRETEND WHAT IS TRUE. Then everything will make sense... If you pretend something that is actually true, then the truth of that experience is automatically drawn into your life."

Who am I? That is the only question we must ask ourselves in life. The discovery of our true essence and identity is the reason for our existence. It should be our only worry, our only goal. It is very important to discover who we are.

Through Ho'oponopono, an ancient Hawaiian art that I now practice and teach,

I learned that our mind consists of three parts: the superconscious, the conscious, and the subconscious. This has helped me to understand a little bit more how we function.

- The superconscious is our spiritual side. It's the part that, no matter what is happening, is always perfect. It's the part that knows, and above all is very clear who it is all the time.

- The conscious part of us is the mental side, what we call the intellect. It's a very important aspect of our being, because it's the one part that has the ability to choose, since we have the gift of free will. In every moment of our lives we are choosing. What are we choosing? We choose if we are going to react and engage when a problem comes up, or if we prefer to let it go and let it be resolved by the part of us that knows better. We also choose, if we are going to accept that we do not know anything (and that we do not need to know), or conversely, if we prefer to think that we know better than God and that we can resolve everything by ourselves. The conscious is the part of us that decides whether to assume 100% of the responsibility by saying, "I'm sorry, please forgive me for whatever is going on in me that has created this," (Ho'oponopono), or to point fingers and blame someone else. The intellect was not created to know. It doesn't need to know anything. The intellect is a gift. The gift that we have to choose.

- The subconscious is our emotional side. It is our inner child. This is the part that stores all our memories. This extremely important part of ourselves is constantly neglected. Despite this, it is responsible for what we manifest in our lives. This is the part that runs our bodies, the one that breathes automatically without us having to "think" about breathing. It's our intuitive side. Have you ever felt nervous but didn't know why? The subconscious alerts us (if we pay attention) when it detects that something bad is about to happen. If we were more connected with it, we could avoid many unpleasant events. This part is the best partner we could have. It is very important that we communicate with it. We must learn to love it and take good care of it. Once we decide to continue on this path of taking responsibility and we are conscious of it, our inner child will erase (Ho'oponopono) for us automatically, without us having to think about it. In the Ho'oponopono classes, we work a lot with this inner child. We learn how to communicate with it, how to take care of it, and above all, how to work with it to "let go."

In the book, *The Teaching of Buddha*, I read, *"Even if a man conquers thousands of men on the battle field, only he who conquers himself will win his battle."*

And one time I read the following story: Once upon a time, in a place that could have been any place, in a time that could have been any time, there was a beautiful garden with apple and orange trees, beautiful roses, all happy and satisfied. Everything was happiness in the garden, except for a tree that was terribly sad. The poor tree had a problem: It didn't know who it was!

"What you lack is concentration," the apple tree would tell it. "If you really tried, you could have delicious apples. See how easy it is." "Don't listen to him," the rose bush would plead. "It's easier to have roses, and look how beautiful we are!" The desperate tree would try everything that they suggested, but since he couldn't be like the rest, every time he would feel more and more frustrated.

One day an owl arrived at the garden, the wisest of all the birds, and at seeing the desperation of the tree exclaimed, "Don't worry. Your problem is not that serious. It's the same as that of many human beings on earth! I will give you the solution: Don't dedicate your life to being what others want you to be. Be yourself. Know yourself, and to do that, listen to your inner voice." And having said that, the owl disappeared.

"My inner voice? Be myself? Know myself?" the desperate tree would ask himself, when suddenly he understood. Closing his ears, he opened his heart and finally heard his inner voice telling him, "You will never give apples because you are not an apple tree, and you will not bloom every spring because you are not a rose bush. You are a redwood, and your destiny is to grow tall and majestic. You are here to give shelter to the birds, shade to the travelers, beauty to the countryside! You have a mission! Go for it!" And the tree felt strong and sure of itself and it set itself out to be all that it was meant to be. In this way it quickly filled its space and was admired and respected by everyone. Only then was the garden completely happy.

As I look around I ask myself, "How many are redwoods that don't allow themselves to grow? How many are rose bushes that for fear only give thorns? How many orange trees are there that don't know how to bloom?" In life we all have a destiny to fulfill, a space to fill up. Let's not let anything or anyone prevent us from knowing and sharing the marvelous essence of our being.

Chapter II

What is a problem?

A problem is only a problem if we say it is, and a problem is not the problem, how we react to the problem is the problem.

— Dr. Ihaleakalá Hew Len

There's a Zen proverb that says, "You cannot stop birds from flying around your heads, but you can prevent them from making nests in your hair."

It's not about denying ourselves or about not giving in to the temptation of paying attention to them. It's about discovering who we are. When we do, we evolve and we feel an inner freedom so that these things can no longer distract us.

Our subconscious has stored all of our memories. While these memories are asleep, arranged in our memory bank, they are not a problem. The people that appear in our lives, the visits to certain places or the situations in life awaken these memories. In that way, the memories convert themselves into thoughts and manifest themselves. That's why it is very important to know that in reality people appear in our lives to give us another opportunity. What is that opportunity? It is to make ourselves one hundred percent responsible and say, "I'm sorry. Please forgive me, for whatever is going on in me that is creating this." (Ho'oponopono)

Have you ever noticed that every time there is a problem you are always there? If the topic had not been inside of you, you would not be capable of perceiving it.

Problems are simply a repetition of our memories. They are like information that is recorded on an audio tape. When the tape begins to play, we think it is real.

Problems repeat themselves because when they appear, we react and hold on to them. We don't stop thinking about the problem, and so we get trapped. We attract even more problems, when we could simply choose to let it go.

Have you noticed that we only think obsessively when a problem arises? Once this vicious cycle begins, we forget that we have the power to stop the recording.

In his book, *The Power Of Now*, Eckhart Tolle says, *"The mind can never find the solution, nor can it permit itself to be found by you, because the mind itself is intrinsically part of the problem."*

Many times the tape is playing but the volume is low. We are not even aware of it. However, the subconscious is always playing the tapes. That's why it is so important to assume one hundred percent responsibility. Only in that way, do we understand that it is just us and our recordings, our thoughts and our programs.

Let's take the example of a slide projected onto the wall or on a screen. We know perfectly well that, even though we see the image projected on the wall or the screen, it is not there but instead inside the machine. The same occurs with our problems. When they appear, they are only a projection of what is going on inside of us and not outside. Despite this, we spend our lives trying to change the screen. The problem is not "out" there. We are always looking for the solution in the wrong place.

It's very important to remember that the problems, the situations, and the people do not exist outside of us like we perceive them, but that our perception is simply a reflection of our thoughts. The problems are not what we think they are either. We never know what is really going on. The problems are "always" opportunities.

We must realize that we have an effect on the event or the problem, and that we have created it. This is, in fact, good news, given that if we are creating it, we can change it without depending on anything or anyone.

There is a story that tells that in a village there was a very poor elder, who was envied even by kings for the beautiful white horse he possessed.

The kings offered him enormous quantities for the horse but the man would say, "For me he is not a horse; he is a person. And how could a person, or a friend, be sold?" He was a poor man, but he never sold his horse. One morning he discovered that the horse was no longer in the stable. The whole village convened saying, "Stupid old man. We knew that some day they would steal your horse. It would have been better if you had sold it. What a shame!"

"Let's not get carried away," said the old man. "Let's just say that the horse is not in the stable. That is the fact. Everything else is your judgment. If it is a misfortune or good luck I do not know, because this is merely a fragment. Who knows what will happen tomorrow?"

The people laughed at him. They had always thought the old man was a bit crazy. But after 15 days, one night the horse returned. He had not been stolen but had escaped. And not only that, but he had brought with him a dozen wild horses. Once again the people convened saying, "You were right old man. It was not a misfortune but good luck instead."

"Once again you are getting carried away," said the old man. "Say only that the horse has returned. Who knows if this is good luck or not? It is only a fragment. You are reading only a word of the sentence. How can you judge the whole book?"

This time the village could say no more, but inside they knew that he was wrong. Twelve beautiful horses had arrived.

The old man had a son who began to train the horses. A week later he fell off a horse and broke both his legs. The people once again convened and judged.

"You were right again," they said. "It was a misfortune. Your only son has lost the use of his legs, and at your age he was your only support. Now you are poorer than ever."

"You are obsessed with judging," said the old man. "Do not get carried away. Say only that my son has broken both his legs. Nobody knows if this is a misfortune or good luck. Life comes in fragments, and we are never given more than that."

A few weeks later, the country went to war and all the young people from the village were called to the army. Only the old man's son was spared because he was injured. The whole village would cry and complain because it was a hopeless war and they knew that most of these young people would not return.

"You were right, old man. It was good fortune. Although crippled, your son is still with you. Ours are gone forever."

"You are still judging," said the old man. Nobody knows. Say only that your sons have been forced to join the army and that my son has not been forced. Only God knows if it is a misfortune or good luck for this to occur."

When we form an opinion or a judgment, we get stuck; we enslave ourselves.

The book, *The Teaching of Buddha*, says, *"He who is influenced by his likes and dislikes cannot understand the significance of the circumstances and tends to despair before them. He who is detached understands perfectly the circumstances and for him all things are new and significant."* Later on it says: *"Happiness follows sadness. Sadness follows happiness, but when one no longer discriminates between happiness and sadness, the good and the bad, one is capable of freeing oneself."*

Nothing is what it seems. The intellect cannot know. Its understanding is limited. However there is a part of us that does know. The difference between intellectual understanding and that innate wisdom that we have is similar to the one that exists between standing on a chair, looking around and thinking that we are seeing everything, and standing at the top of a mountain and seeing the whole picture. We prefer to talk with our psychologists or with our neighbors instead of talking to God. We have permanent access to all this knowledge, to all this wisdom that is inside of us, but we prefer to stand on a chair and spout opinions, make judgments and express our point of view because that is what we learned to do. We are addicted to this manner of operating.

Nevertheless, we can always choose what to do and how to react when a situation appears that we consider problematic. The following story beautifully illustrates this concept, *"One day a farmer's donkey fell to the bottom of a well. The animal cried piteously for hours while the farmer tried to find a way to get it out. Finally, the farmer decided that the animal was old, and that the well needed to be covered up anyway. It was not worth it to get the donkey out. Therefore, the farmer invited his neighbors to help him out. Everyone took a shovel and began to throw dirt into the well. In the beginning, when the donkey realized what was happening, it cried piteously. But after a while, to the surprise of everyone, it calmed down. After many shovels of dirt, the farmer finally decided to look inside the pit, and he was astonished at what he saw. With every shovel of dirt that fell on its back, the donkey would do something amazing. It would shake it off and take a step up. As the farmer's neighbors continued to throw dirt onto the animal, it would shake it off and take a step up. Very soon, the donkey reached the border of the well and took off with a trot."*

Life is going to shovel dirt on you, all kinds of dirt. The trick to getting out of the well is shaking it off, and taking a step up. Each of our troubles is a stepping stone.

We can get out of the deepest wells just by not giving up! Shake it off and take a step up!

Chapter III

Faith?

Our true power is happiness,
and this comes only when we
surrender everything else.

– *Dan Millman*

"*Way of the Peaceful Warrior*"

Most of my life I did not believe in God. God did not exist for me. I grew up thinking that I was the one that achieved everything in my life and that everything I had I owed to my work, dedication and personal effort. We, Jews, are very traditional, and I, like a good Jew, respected these traditions. But I did not believe in God. When I finally woke up, I discovered inside myself a new world that I was completely unfamiliar with. A little later I told my oldest son, "Jonathan, life can be easy." He looked at me completely confused and said, "That's not what you used to tell me before," to which I answered, "I know. But now I know better." At that moment I didn't have the slightest doubt. It was an intangible feeling that could not be expressed with words, I found it in my heart. We can all find it because we carry it within us. Like a good accountant, I look at the results, I observe, and when I look back on my life since my awakening, it seems unbelievable all that has happened to me.

Some find God in a temple or church. Others, like me, do not find it there. One day we wake up, we start to look and we realize that it is not even necessary to rise from bed to find God. It doesn't matter the denomination, or what we call God, He (She) is always with us. Wherever we go, He (She) accompanies us.

We do not know, nor do we have the slightest idea, how God (Love) works. We don't know what it can do for us. We cannot even imagine it. The so called miracles do really exist. We can experience them in every moment of our lives if we stop trying to understand everything with the intellect, and if we let go of our judgments and opinions, and learn to let ourselves be taken by the flow of life. It is necessary to become aware that we, ourselves, are our own greatest obstacles in our own lives!

We say that we trust but we don't really. We say that we give our problems to God (Love) but we still hold on to them. When we don't stop thinking about them, and we get upset and worry, we let God (Love) know that we want to solve everything alone because we do not have faith in Him (Her). In that way, we do not get answers to our prayers because we have "expectations." We believe that we know what is right and perfect for us, and when we ask something of God, we do it in an almost commanding way. We tell Him (Her) what we want, how, what color and at what time we want it. However, God knows before we ask. He (She) is so close that we do not need to shout.

It is sufficient to think it. God has much more for us than we can imagine. He (She) is only waiting for us to give Him (Her) permission to give it to us. If we ask for specific things, like for example, "Oh God, I would like to have money to travel to Europe," we put limits on our request. God grants us what is correct in every moment. In the case of the example, perhaps the correct thing for me was to go to South America instead of Europe, but in being so closed off, the money does not come because what I requested is not correct for me. Maybe I was going to have an accident and die in Europe. In closing ourselves off in this manner, we are left without the possibility of receiving what is correct and perfect in a given moment. Sometimes God says no, like a good parent does when his/her child cannot measure or realize the danger or the consequences of what he/she is asking for. For this reason, the secret is in requesting what is correct and perfect, and we do not know what that is. It is necessary to let go of expectations. In the precise moment the most appropriate and perfect thing will arrive. We never know where it will come from. To receive the surprise, we must give permission.

God (Love) works in mysterious ways. If we allow it, if we believe and trust with all our hearts, everything will come to us without effort. God is the only one that can open certain doors and bring us close to the people who can help us and support us on our path. He (She) puts us in the correct place in the perfect moment only when we stop talking so much to our neighbor instead of asking Him (Her) directly.

Just thinking about God lifts us away from our problems. Also, being thankful for what we have automatically changes our vibration. There are always good reasons to be thankful.

The Indigo Children say, "If you imagine and believe that something will happen, it happens. If you imagine it but you don't believe it, it will be difficult for it to happen." It's about having faith and not 'waiting for' or 'wishing' for something to happen. Having faith is being open to the possibilities. It means that we are willing to allow life to surprise us, that we dare to enter into the unknown and to stop being afraid of what appears uncertain to us. Whenever someone has faith, his/her heart opens. Many times we remain stuck and go around in circles in the same place for lack of faith and fear of the unknown. It is worth it to learn from the seed, which despite its inability to imagine itself an orchid, has the courage to open, get broken, and give itself to the process entirely to sprout from the earth's surface and emerge to the light. A heart full of pain cannot imagine what it feels like to be loved or to be at peace. And that is how it is with everything. Many times we have to break with old patterns, old ways of thinking, and old beliefs. This implies having to pass through a dark tunnel, and at times having to feel pain, but it is the only way to come out ahead and to see the light.

Jesus said that we must be like children to be able to enter into the kingdom of heaven. The kingdom of heaven is here and now. It is dependent on us to experience it. We only have to stop thinking so much and stop believing that we know everything and we are always right. Many times, all our thoughts, information, and education distance us from what we really are. Innocence is no more than God's wisdom in us.

Of course it is necessary to be brave to take this path, but victory is one hundred percent assured. It is necessary to dare to believe, try, trust, and surrender. When we begin to trust and have faith, something inside of us transforms and our thinking clears up. Everything looks different. We try to explain this transformation with words, but it is not possible. There are no words to define it. We only know that we have found the wisdom of the heart.

Now I would like to discuss the most important kind of faith, faith in oneself. It is not imperative to believe in anything outside ourselves. It is not necessary to believe in God, Jesus, Buddha, or Moses, unless this makes us feel good. What is necessary is to believe and trust ourselves and in the power that is inside of us. To reach it, we must renounce many beliefs, opinions, and judgments about ourselves, in order to like and accept ourselves exactly the way we are. I know that this is not easy. We do not even consciously know what these beliefs are that affect us, but with the process that I teach in this book, it is not necessary to know them, just to give permission for them to go away.

When we believe in ourselves and we love ourselves unconditionally, we become invincible. People perceive this quality. It is not necessary to speak or to say anything. When we believe in ourselves, we will notice that certain people begin to distance from us while others come closer, bringing with them the opportunities we yearn for. The secret lies in accepting ourselves just the way we are, no longer believing that we are not good, that we are not intelligent enough, that we do not have enough money, or that a university degree is necessary first to be worthy. Only we can change what we believe about ourselves.

The most important thing is to put ourselves first in order to stop being that person that others want us to be. It is necessary to wake up and understand that the power is inside of us and not in the approval of others. When we have faith in ourselves, our inner talents automatically begin to grow and we begin to feel happy. Faith in ourselves has to do with the capacity to love and to enjoy life.

Our lives go by in our own minds. The war is inside our heads and only we can return the peace. It is essential to remember that in one sense we are always right. If we say we can, we can. If we say we cannot, that's how it is, we cannot. We are here to live, enjoy life, and be happy. Faith in ourselves gives us the freedom to be authentic, and this in turn begets the happiness that we yearn for so much.

Chapter IV

Money

Even when we attain all our desired possessions, we soon find that the hole is still there, that it is bottomless.

— *Eckhart Tolle*
"The Power of Now"

When I separated from my husband after
twenty years of marriage, I left only with
what I had on. I didn't even take my kids.
Their father chose to stay with them. I
had the certainty that I could go on alone
and I was grateful and happy to have the
opportunity to begin anew. On the other
hand, at that stage of my life I had learned
that happiness is not in the material things
and that I did not need possessions. On the
contrary, the less I had, the freer I would be.

A friend suggested that we move together in order to find a nicer and bigger place. This seemed like a good idea, and that is how we found a beautiful townhouse. I never imagined that we would fulfill the requirements to rent it, but because we demonstrated that we had two incomes, we were approved.

Two days before signing the lease, my friend called me and told me that she had changed her mind and that she was going to live in Arizona. I immediately called the real estate agent to ask that the contract be changed to my name, and I told her that I would make myself the responsible party. She had no problem doing this because she already knew me.

Not long after signing the year long lease and moving into the house, I started getting work from everywhere and I soon realized that I could pay the rent without any problem and that I didn't need to share my house with another person.

Eight months after moving, the owner of the house called me and said that he wished to sell the property. He explained that since he knew I liked the house he wanted to give me priority, but that if I was not interested, I would have to be out of there in September.

Of course I wanted to buy the property and stay there, but with what? I didn't have money for the down payment, and since I'm an accountant, I knew very well that I did not have the necessary requisites to get a loan. My intellect was telling me to start packing, but something inside of me was saying that it was not the best option. In that moment I said to myself, "If God thinks this is the place for me, He will find me the loan, because I don't know how to do it." I knew that I needed to get out of the way and give permission. The best thing was to let go, trust, and hand over the matter to the universe.

Two people who had told me that they might be able to help me to get the loan gave up the process. The lease expired and I did not get the loan, so I had to call the owner to tell him what was happening. I decided that instead of worrying about what I would say and what I would do to convince him, I would surrender to the situation with confidence and faith. And so I called him and explained everything to him, and surprisingly he answered, "Okay Mabel, in truth this is not the right time to put the property up for sale. I will extend the lease. Write an extension, fax it to me, and I will sign it."

In the end I didn't even have to call the person who got me the loan. George called me to offer his help, and before the extension expired he got me the loan! Thanks George!

When we stop attaching ourselves to the result and worrying about situations, when we abandon the need to have opinions and pass judgment, and when we become conscious that we don't know anything and we surrender and accept the process of life, only then, can we experience the flow of life.

Then everything will happen, and things will come to us in the easiest way. God has put us on earth with everything that we need. If we look around us we can see that everything created by God is infinite and abundant. Only human creations are scarce and limited. Birds fly untroubled knowing that they will find what they need to eat nearby, close to where they find themselves.

Manifesting that which we desire requires much TRUST and CONFIDENCE. The universe only needs us to take that first step. If we trust and give our permission, everything that we need comes to us easily. The important thing is to know in our hearts (and not in our heads) that God will provide, and to trust one hundred percent. When we think that we are not receiving answers to our prayers or we don't see results, it is not because we are not heard. Many times we think of God as our servant and we demand what we want, how, what color, and at what time. That is not how the universe works. It is necessary to ask without having expectations, asking for that which we think is correct for us and then letting go. God gives us what is correct and perfect in every moment. The secret is to TRUST and let go, letting ourselves be taken by the flow of life and being open to receiving from the place and person we least expected.

Our problem is that we have expectations, we want things in advance and we are very impatient and inflexible. We do not realize that everything comes from only ONE SOURCE that knows exactly what we need, how and when we need it. We think we are the ones creating the opportunities through our work, our spouses, our investments, but all these are different ways and roads through which things manifest. When a door closes, it is because another is going to open automatically.

The worst thing that we can do when a problem arises is to worry. In doing this, we get stuck and trap ourselves, and we end up attracting more of precisely what we don't

want. We are like magnets: Tell me what
you think and I will tell you who you are.
It is of vital importance to live in the NOW.
We spend our existence living in the past
with our memories and experiences or in
the future with our worries. Money, like
everything else, comes when we need it, not
before or after. It is only necessary to open
our hearts and TRUST.

Someone once told me the following story:
A woman went out of her home and saw
three old men with long beards sitting in
front of her garden. Since she didn't know
them, she said, "I don't think I know you,
but perhaps you are hungry. Please come
into my home and eat something." They
asked her, "Is the man of the house home?"
"No," she answered, "he is not here." "Then
we cannot go inside," they told her. In the
evening, when her husband returned home,
the woman told him what had happened.
He said, "Tell them that I have arrived and
invite them to come in!" The woman went
outside to invite the men in. "All three of

us cannot go in at once," explained the old men. "Why?" she wanted to know. In that moment, one of the men pointed towards the other two and said, "His name is Wealth and his name is Success. My name is Love. Go inside and decide with your husband which one of the three of us you would like to invite in." The woman went inside her home and repeated the story to her husband. The man became very happy. "Fantastic! Since that is the case, let's invite Wealth in. Let him come in and fill our home with abundance." The wife did not agree. "Honey, why don't we invite in Success?" The couple's daughter, who was listening to the conversation from the other end of the house, came running up with an idea. "Wouldn't it be better to invite Love? Then our home would be filled with Love." "Let's listen to our daughter," the man told his wife. "Go invite Love to be our guest." The woman went outside and asked the three men, "Which one of you is Love? We wish for him to be our guest." Love stood up and started to walk towards the house. The other two old men stood up and followed him. Surprised, the woman asked them, "I only invited in Love. Why are you also coming?" The old men responded in unison, "If you had invited in Wealth or Success, the other two would have stayed outside. But you invited Love, and wherever Love goes, we go." Where there is love, there is also wealth and success.

Money is not bad; on the contrary, the bad thing is to put it first. When we do things for the money, everything seems difficult. It comes and goes quickly and it escapes from our hands. We must find what we love to do, something that brings us happiness and satisfaction and that we would be willing to do even if we don't get paid for. We are all born with certain talents and unique natural gifts. There is something that we can do better than anyone else. It is something that is inside of us and that doesn't necessarily come from a university degree.

Abundance and prosperity have to do with our consciousness. When we know who we are, we know that we already have everything that we need. In that moment we are already rich. When we open our hearts and trust, we give permission for everything to manifest in our lives.

Chapter V

Fears

*And the truth will set
you free.*
– Jesus

In this path of spiritual searching that I have decided to take, I had to face many of my fears. I felt fear when I left my marriage of more than twenty years, leaving my children, starting my career anew, and in signing a lease where I assumed all the responsibility without having any financial backing. However, faith and confidence in myself allowed me to act in spite of my fear. An inner voice told me that I could do it. But this security did not come by itself; I acquired it by working on myself reading books, taking seminars, daring to face and accept the things that I needed to change. I learned a lot from experiences like Rebirthing and the Sweat Lodge.

Inside a Sweat Lodge it is pitch black and extremely hot. The heat is so intense that it hurts your chest when you breathe and you feel like you are going to die. The American Indian who was leading the experience in Mount Shasta, explained to us that in the Sweat Lodge one has no other option than to give in and see oneself. I remember having two very important thoughts there: "If God allows me to do this it must be safe," and immediately afterwards I told myself, "Mabel, if you can do this, you can do anything." I think that I left many of my fears in that Sweat Lodge.

When we discover who we are and the power that we possess, we understand that there is nothing to fear. We are always taken care of. We are always protected.

We all suffer from fear, we could even say it is an illness.

We are addicted to fear, to suffering. We prefer to suffer because it is familiar. We know how it feels. Despite our suffering, we feel comfortable. Fear is a familiar, everyday thing.

When we dare to face and go through our fears, we reach the other side of the tunnel. We see the light. We recognize what is true and, not only do we feel triumphant and very happy with ourselves, but we look back and see that it wasn't as terrible as we had imagined.

I once took a business class where a certain person told us the story of how he had become a real estate agent. He was very young, and on his first day on the job his boss had asked him, "Do you want to sell houses?" Of course, he immediately answered that he did. The boss took him to a neighborhood and told him, "This is where

I am going to leave you. I will pick you up in four hours. Go and knock door to door and ask the people if they want to sell their homes." He left him a paper with a grid with one hundred boxes and told him that every time someone said no, he should make an X in one of the boxes. "Go and look for your first hundred NOs." The young man could not believe it, but there was no way out of the situation. As it turned out many did say NO, but to his surprise, many said YES - that they had just been thinking about it and they wanted to get more information. In that moment the young man realized that with every person who said NO, he got closer to the possibility of a YES.

We all have a big fear of NO, a great fear of rejection. But if we don't risk receiving a NO, we will never receive the YES. What happens if people say no to us? If we really think about it, it's not that terrible.

The capacity to overcome fear is what differentiates the people that get a lot out of life from those that hardly get anything at all, the people that are successful and excel from those that stay stuck.

Fear has to do with our own insecurities. We don't know who we are, nor do we know the power or ability we have to attract all that is perfect and correct for ourselves. When we trust and believe in ourselves, we know how to recognize that every moment is perfect. If someone tells us NO, it's not a big deal, since perhaps what we were looking for was not perfect and correct for us in that moment. When we love and accept ourselves, we do not depend on what other people say or think of us. We do not take it personally.

He who has faith, knows that many times in these moments, something bigger and better is on its way, and awaits it with certainty and confidence. On the other hand, he who is lost and confused and does not know his true identity feels a deep paralyzing fear.

We all feel fear, from the person that sweeps the streets to the president of a nation. Fears do not have a hierarchy. The difference is that some people dare to feel them and go through them anyway.

It is necessary to be brave in order to realize these changes. But if we don't do it, no one will do it for us. Neither Jesus nor Buddha will return to save us. What we need in order to transform ourselves is inside of us. The transformation is an internal one. There is no other way to do it. There is no short cut in this search. Each one of us chooses our own path. The braver we are, the farther we go and the more possibilities that present themselves in our path. The good news is that fears exist only in our minds. They are created by us. Only we can change them. Beliefs and memories can be erased. We do not need them to survive. Our freedom depends on this process. In abandoning the prison that we have created in our minds, we are opening the door to our soul and recovering our freedom.

Fear and suffering, much like bravery, are optional. They depend only on what we choose each moment. Many times it is necessary to stop in the middle of the road and make drastic changes. In some ways, we must die first in order to start to live. I speak of the death of that part of ourselves that is not real, of that which we believed we were, of the image that we sold to others, and worse yet, that we sold to ourselves.

Fear assumes something bad will happen, knowing that the bad things we imagine will actually happen. Fear also moves mountains.

I once read that success in life is not measured by what we have accomplished, but by the obstacles that we have had to face.

Many times happiness is just around the corner, on that corner that we never dare to turn.

Chapter VI

Love

Love is the sword of the soldier: wherever it cuts, it gives life, not death.
– Dan Millman
   "Way of the Peaceful Warrior"

When someone asked one of the Indigo Girls to tell them about love, she laughed as though they had asked her a strange question and then responded, "I can't tell you about love; if I could, then it wouldn't be real, because love has nothing to do with words." "So then," the person insisted, "what is real love?" She laughed again and said, "You have done it again. See how difficult it is?"

It doesn't matter how much we try not to think, it is almost impossible. We are always trying to understand everything with our intellect and then we want this understanding to flow from our mouths. But the mind cannot understand love because it has nothing to do with "thinking."

Dan Millman, in his book, Way of the Peaceful Warrior, says, "Love cannot be understood, it must be felt. Life is not imagining perfection and triumph, it is only love. We always try to change everything into a mental concept. Forget that, just feel!"

One day I told my children, Jonathan and Lyonel, that I loved them no matter what. That my love didn't depend on what they did or didn't do, nor on their behavior, and that it didn't depend on whether or not they got a college degree. They opened their eyes wide and looked at me as though I was telling them the strangest thing they had ever heard in their lives.

We have many bad habits, and we transmit our habits to our children. This is how we learn to live. We don't know a better way. Beginning in childhood, we are taught that we must do things or behave in a certain way to get love and acceptance from others. But unfortunately in that process we don't learn to love and accept ourselves. And paradoxically, people treat us in the same way that we treat ourselves. In this way, the desire for love and acceptance is obstructed by our own incapacity to love ourselves.

Without self love, we cannot love anyone else. By not accepting this truth we are deceiving ourselves and deceiving others. The essential thing is to learn to love and to accept ourselves exactly the way we are. It doesn't work to do things for others. If something doesn't work for us, it won't work for them. Especially us mothers, we tend to believe that we have to relinquish what is important to us and sacrifice for our children. However, the best gift that we can give to our children is to love ourselves. In this way they can observe, and by our example, learn to love themselves without needing to look for love in the wrong places. When we are in the correct place, we allow for others to be at their correct place.

The more we try to have love by doing things and behaving in certain ways for others, the more we distance ourselves from the possibility of experiencing that thing that we so much desire. We must learn to be happy and to enjoy every moment of our lives without placing importance on what others think of us. The most important thing is what we think of ourselves. Love towards our own being is the most powerful tool of transformation. Love begins with us. It is useless to look for it outside. It does not exist. We spend most of our time looking for love in the wrong place, always begging for it from others without knowing why.

Another terrible mistake that we all tend to commit, is thinking that in order to be happy we must have a partner. We think that the other person will give us the happiness that we so yearn for. But even when we find someone to love us, we are not happy. We feel that we are not complete, and we look for what we think is lacking in ourselves in the other person. This is a waste of time. We must find Love inside ourselves. Once we have found it, once we feel good with ourselves, once we accept and love ourselves just the way we are, we discover that in reality one does not "need" anyone. Finally, we begin to look for someone because we "want to" and "choose to" be in a relationship, not because we "need to." In this context one acts freely by choice and not by necessity.

Because we lack trust in ourselves, we cannot love truthfully. We say we do, but we love possessively. For example, as mothers, we don't allow our kids to be themselves and they are slaves of our thoughts, opinions and perceptions. Sometimes we create relationships where we feel a lot of jealousy. This is not Love, but we cannot help it. They are those old tapes playing again in our heads. We don't actually see people as they are, we see them through our thoughts and memories.

The Hawaiian art of Ho'oponopono uses two very important tools: the words "I love you" and "thank you." When we use them aloud and say them to someone, they are tremendously powerful and valuable. Sometimes, even if you do not feel like it, you will find it extremely powerful to do the following: when someone does something you consider unfair, when someone says something that bothers you, instead of answering them, instead of giving them a piece of your mind and trying to convince them that you are right, you can repeat in your mind as many times as necessary, "I love you. I love you. I love you," or "Thank you, Thank you. Thank you." These tools often bring about surprising results. Sometimes the person asks for forgiveness when we least expect it.

Other times, things remain the same, but we no longer notice or are affected by them. With certain people, the difficulties are less severe than with others. With some people we have more stories, more tapes. We must not forget that everything changes according to our perception of events, people, and situations. The same happens to everyone. Everything depends on their perception, their point of view, and their memories. Life is like a movie that we have already seen many times and that keeps repeating itself over because we keep on reacting every time it plays.

Our reaction to problems is a repetition of memories. Problems are often obstacles that we have already encountered, but that we have never resolved. For this reason, the situation returns to give us the opportunity to react in a different way. People often come into our lives in order to show us the parts of ourselves that we need to work on. Relationships are simply mirrors in which we see ourselves reflected. We have the option to choose not to react. We can turn the other cheek. The cheek of Love. Knowing this, we can become conscious and choose to make ourselves responsible. For example, if someone has problems with their children, the best thing to do is talk to them when they are asleep. The only thing you need to tell them is that you love them and that you are grateful to them for being in your life. It is not proper to tell them your point of view unless they ask for it. It is not productive to try to convince them that you are right and they are wrong. It is very difficult to know what is right for ourselves. How can we possibly know what is right for others?

Gratitude is also a very powerful tool. When we feel depressed or sorrowful, the best thing to do is to think about all the good things in our lives we can be grateful for. By doing that, we will change our energy very quickly. We elevate ourselves and we are higher than our problems. Sometimes we don't realize everything that we have because we concentrate instead on what we "think" is missing. In truth we already have everything, including love. We only have to give our permission to receive it and therefore be able to experience it.

The secret to happiness is not in looking outside, or in looking for more. It is in developing our capacity to love and enjoy ourselves more.

Chapter VII

The shortest and easiest way

The only thing God is asking from us is that we take good care of ourselves and that we say "I am sorry."

– Dr. Ihaleakalá Hew Len

When I woke up and began my search, I tried different ways and paths to get to the truth. The more I tried, the more I felt that something inside of me was saying that there had to be a faster and easier way. When I finally discovered Ho'oponopono, I did not realize immediately what I had found. I took the training several times, and one day while in a class taught by my teacher Ihaleakalá, I realized that this was what I had been searching for. I didn't need anything else. Thank God my search had ended. First and foremost, I discovered that I neither needed nor depended on any guru. I can carry out the process alone because I communicate directly with Divinity, without intermediaries. The only things required are to clean and to erase (I am sorry, please forgive me). While I am taking 100% responsibility and cleaning, I am leaving everything in God's hands. As long as I am cleaning, I will not have reason to worry. God makes sure to put me in the right place at the perfect time. As long as I am cleaning, there will be someone to take care of me. I don't need to do it.

In this last chapter, I would like to summarize the most important points of Ho'oponopono, the wise ancient doctrine that has given me the tools that have changed my life. These concepts are very simple. The only thing that Divinity asks of us is that we assume all responsibility, that we ask forgiveness, and that we take good care of ourselves. That is all!

Taking one hundred percent responsibility is the shortest way. When we realize that it is only "our programs" that do not allow us to see things clearly, when we stop blaming outside factors and we decide to take responsibility, only then will heaven's doors open up for us and we can reach a state of infinite possibilities. On the other hand, when we are upset with someone or about something we lose our freedom. Our own feelings of hate condemn us and tie us down. We are slaves to them. We only hurt ourselves in this manner. We can free ourselves through forgiveness. Forgiveness is a part of the shortest and easiest way. But it is not necessary to speak with anyone to let them know that we have forgiven them. This is an internal job. It is a process that takes place between us and God when we say, "I am sorry, please forgive me for what is going on in me that has created this situation/problem."

In my case, for example, it's not that I no longer get angry; it's not that I no longer react or have problems. The big difference is that now my anger lasts only a few minutes until I return to my center, until I remind myself and become aware. Then I tell myself, "I am creating this. They are my thoughts of the other person. It is a product of my own programming, my recordings, my perception. I can erase it." This simple process gives me a peace that I can't describe with words. Why? Because I don't stay trapped in thoughts like, "How could he say that to me? How could she do that to me?" I don't expect the other person to change, react in a specific way or do something specific. What a relief! I don't depend on anyone or anything outside of myself. I don't expect myself to be perfect, or to please the whole world. I don't need to convince anyone of my point of view. I learned to respect and understand that we all have free will and not all of us choose the same things. This reality brings me a lot of inner peace. There is no problem. Good and bad are parameters that we create in our minds. As long as we love ourselves and take care of ourselves, we will love and take care of others as well.

So then, what are the keys to this freeing process?

First and foremost it is necessary to take complete responsibility for our lives. We have to learn to say, "I'm sorry, please forgive me for whatever is going on in me that is creating this." In this way we take responsibility, and from there the process of forgiveness and transmutation begins. We are forgiving ourselves. Since we have memories in common, it is enough for you to take the responsibility of asking for forgiveness for those memories to be erased. When they get erased from your consciousness, they get erased from the others as well. However, it is important to remember that when you do this cleaning, you do it for yourself, not for others. We are here to save ourselves and nobody else, but the beauty of this process is that it benefits everyone.

It is also important to surrender and accept that the intellect doesn't know anything, but that there is a part of us that knows what is perfect and right for us and the best way to achieve it. If we allow it to do that, that part that does know will guide us to find the right and perfect solution for all our problems.

In order to see the results of this "cleaning" it is important to do it all the time, like breathing. Do you know what happens if we forget to breathe? The same occurs with this cleaning. It has to be done all the time. Of course we are human beings and many times we will forget. Other times we won't be able to help it and we will react. The important thing is to practice this method as much as possible, even when it "looks like" nothing is happening, or when problems do not appear to be arising. Why? Because the mind plays the tapes all the time. It permanently repeats the programs that we have recorded, even if we are not aware of it. Luckily, we always have the possibility to erase it. This way we give permission for new ideas and opportunities to appear in our lives. Many times these will come from the people and places we would least expect it. It is necessary to practice, practice, practice. Throughout our entire lives we have practiced reacting and suffering. We have incorporated reacting and suffering so far into our lives that we do it almost automatically. We are experts, masters, and I would even say we are addicted to this way of living. In the beginning cleaning might seem difficult. But we learn to incorporate it into our daily life like breathing, and it becomes automatic because we begin to feel different and we see the results. We begin to see changes in our lives. We begin to experience a profound inner peace.

It is important not to have expectations. The secret is in being open and flexible, because we never know where it is going to come from. We have to trust that the right thing for us will come. Perhaps it won't be what we were expecting, but it will be the right thing. This is not because we were not heard, because it is a test, or because we did not deserve it. We have to allow ourselves to be surprised by the universe. In that way we receive the most incredible gifts. The law of the universe is that when we ask, we receive. The universe has to respond. It is necessary to ask and to give permission. One way of asking is by using the tools of Ho'oponopono. But we have to detach ourselves from the result. This is done by knowing and trusting that the right and perfect thing for us will come.

Now then, there are many tools to erase the programs that our mind repeats. I am sharing the basic and most important ones here: "thank you" and "I love you." For example, all you need is to just repeat mentally, "thank you, thank you, thank you," all the time. With these words we stop the tapes and we allow God to take care of us and our problems.

Many times people tell me, "How can I pay attention when people talk to me if I am thinking, 'thank you'?" In the first place, it is important to remember that people almost never say what they really mean. If someone tells us their problem, they are only doing it to give us the opportunity to erase and clean the memories that we have in common. Remember that they are only our screens, our monitors. Next time, before reacting, before giving advice or opinions, think "I love you" or "Thank you." Most likely you will end up saying exactly what that person needed to hear instead of what you thought they needed to hear. Many times it is not even necessary to talk, to answer, or to say anything in order for the person to end up feeling better, or suddenly, in a miraculous way, to end up finding the answer to their problem all by themselves.

"I love you" and "Thank you" are the passwords. When I am worried about my children, anxious about money, or resentful towards someone, I don't allow my intellect to impose itself and start the chatter. I mentally repeat "I love you, I love you, I love you."

I don't have even the slightest doubt that it works, but it is essential to remember that if we decide to try it, different persons have different experiences. Maybe we will see immediate results. Maybe they will take some time. Maybe we won't "become aware" of anything until long after it has happened.

I once told my 16 year old son Lyonel that when he got hurt he could simply think, "Thank you." One day we were having breakfast and he showed me that he had gotten hurt. I asked him, "Lyonel, did you say "thank you"?" His answer was, "Yes Mom. And you know what? When I'm feeling frustrated or anxious I also use it and it really calms me down." In that moment I remembered that "thank you" can be used for any kind of suffering, whether it be physical or emotional.

Another time I said to my son, "Lyonel, I know I talk about things that sound kind of weird, but they really work." He answered,

"Yes mom, of course they work. Remember when you told me what I had to do in school? Well, after I did it, I started getting better grades." A little while ago Lyonel told me that he could not believe how well he was getting along with all his teachers.

It is worth mentioning at this time that physical problems, illnesses, are also memories that can be erased and cleaned. We are used to treating pain or physical maladies, but that is not where the problem lies. The problem is in the memory, the tape is playing! How do we know in which one? How do we find it? Well, we do not need to know which memory or which recording, because God (Love) knows. It's only necessary to give permission. For example by repeating thank you, or I love you, then God can remove the tape or the program that contains those memories and others that are also on that same tape, even if we do not even know they are there. But we must give permission. If not, God cannot do anything.

My son Jonathan fought constantly with his girlfriend. I suggested that the next time they had a fight, he could choose to keep his mouth shut, stay quiet and mentally repeat the words "I love you." A few days later, he called me and said he needed to talk to me. He told me that he had some trouble with his girlfriend, but that this time he was very concerned because he felt like he wanted to hit her. I asked him, "Did you say I love you?" His answer was, "Yes mom, and that's what stopped me."

Undoubtedly some people will think that this is too easy, that it can't be. Yes, I agree, it sounds easy and it is easy. The process itself is very easy. The hard part is doing it all the time. In each moment of our lives we have the chance to take 100% responsibility and to erase our programming. But generally we react, we worry, we have opinions and judgments. By doing this we waste time and energy. It is enough just to remember that problems are not really problems. The way in which we react to them is the problem.

Opinions and judgments that we have about the problem are the true problem. Our perception of the problem is the problem.

The worst part about this is that every time that we decide to react instead of letting go, we sacrifice our true identity, our true being, and we do it simply because of that habit of ours of always wanting to be right. Dead right.

We only have two choices: living according to our true being or according to our tapes, letting ourselves be guided by divine inspiration or by our old programs that we tried before and didn't work. The more that we erase, the more we begin to have the experience of who we really are. The only reason of our existence in this world is to discover who we are. Through the cleaning we do using the tools of Ho'oponopono, we can discover our true identity.

I want to make clear that by using any of these tools we are taking one hundred percent responsibility and we are implicitly saying, "I'm sorry, please forgive me for whatever is inside of me that is causing this." We are asking and letting go and letting God.

So why do we clean? Why do we ask for forgiveness? Because we want to be free, because we are tired of living the lies we have chosen to believe, because we have suffered enough. It is time to find ourselves, to discover ourselves, to be happy, to enjoy life, to love ourselves and accept ourselves just as we are.

The human condition is to be happy. Have you noticed that when we are happy everything comes easy?

The journey is long. We have a lot to clean, a lot to erase. It's a job that must be done 24 hours a day, but the rewards are immeasurable. In the process we can experience love, we can enjoy life, and we can discover that we are already perfect beings. We can attract everything we need without any effort. We can learn to be ourselves and to love unconditionally.

We can choose suffering or happiness, sickness or health, fear or love. Whatever we decide, it will be okay. It will be our choice.

Take good care of yourselves.
Receive all my love.

Appendix

The Easiest Way
to Understanding
Ho'oponopono

The Clearest Answers to Your
Most Frequently Asked Questions

by Mabel Katz

A Note from Mabel

As I travel around the world presenting Ho'oponopono, I realize we all have the same questions and concerns. And I know that some of the information out there isn't very clear and is creating some confusion.

I also know that the only way we are going to unlearn everything we have learned and deprogram everything we have been programmed is by listening and re-listening, reading and re-reading. In my own experience, my intellect needed to understand a little bit to be willing to let go.

As you already know, I love questions because it gives me the opportunity to come from Inspiration.

So I've decided to put together some answers to those questions that have been asked often during Ho'oponopono trainings all over the world.

I hope this will help answer your questions and clarify some of your doubts, and that it will help you do more cleaning. If you aren't sure what cleaning is, it's explained in this book.

I know when you practice Ho'oponopono you'll see the results and we'll all benefit. With Ho'oponopono, you will learn to take 100 percent responsibility.

Ho'oponopono helps you let go of what it is not you, so that you can find out who you really are and fall in love with yourself. Only when you love and accept yourself, can you love and accept others.

As you find yourself, you will find your passion. As you find your passion and trust, you will find your purpose. When you find your purpose and do what you love, the money will come.

As you do what you love, you will be happy. You will find yourself at the right place at the right time, and others will be able to do the same.

You will find out that 100% responsibility is *The Easiest Way* to Peace, Happiness, Love, Wealth and Success.

What is Ho'oponopono?

Ho'oponopono is an ancient Hawaiian art of problem solving.

The original Hawaiians used to practice this. Dr. Ihaleakalá Hew Len, my Ho'oponopono teacher, says that these Hawaiians came from other galaxies.

Many religions are practiced in Hawaii as everywhere else, so not everyone in Hawaii practices Ho'oponopono. Some people in Hawaii have never heard of it.

Morrnah Simeona (Ihaleakalá's teacher) brought these teachings to us and updated them for modern times.

In the past you needed the whole family present, and one by one they would ask for forgiveness from each other. Now we know there is no one else out there. It is just our thoughts of the other person, our own memories of the other person. So we take 100% responsibility and clean those memories. Whatever gets erased from us gets erased from the other people, our family, relatives and ancestors, and the earth. It gets erased from everything. You do not need to be in the presence of others to ask for their forgiveness, now you can do it in your own home. Memories are all inside of us, as we clean, whatever comes off of us, will come off of them without the need to be in their presence.

Ho'oponopono means "to make it right," "to correct an error."

Everything that shows up in our life is a memory, a program playing (an error) and it shows up in our life to give us an opportunity to let go, to clean, to delete.

Ho'oponopono is the delete key on the keyboard of our computer.

See, when you misspell a word, you don't talk to the monitor and tell the monitor "How many times did I tell you how to spell that word?" You know the monitor can't do anything about it. You can talk to the monitor all day long, but the monitor looks at you, like: what does she want me to do?

If you want to change something, you need to delete first, create that empty space in order to put in the right information.

Ho'oponopono takes us back to the void, to zero, so that Inspiration can show up in our life and guide us. That way we can be at the right time at the right place.

What does it mean to be 100% responsible?

You are attracting everything in your life. You don't realize it, but the memories playing inside of you attract everything in your life. You hold data, programs, information, memories that you have accumulated since the beginning of creation. Therefore you're responsible for all your memories that replay as problems that you experience. You were created perfect. You are perfect. Perfect means no memories, no beliefs, no attachments, no judgments. But the memories are not perfect, and many of your memories come from your ancestors. Nothing is what you think it is.

Where do my problems come from?

Most of our problems come from our ancestors. For example, if you know diabetes runs in your family, you would say: "Oh, I know I will have diabetes because it will come down the line through my family." However, you can erase the diabetes before you get it. The same thing with emotional problems or lack of money or relationship challenges. Most of our memories come from our ancestors.

What does "cleaning" mean?

Cleaning means when a problem comes up, you are willing to take 100% responsibility. You are willing to say "I am sorry. Please forgive me for whatever is in me that is attracting this." You can use any cleaning tool that you have. You can also get your own cleaning tools through Inspiration. Cleansing is a petition to Divinity to correct errors from the past. It's a way of giving permission to Divinity to erase whatever is not working and that we are ready to let go. God knows what we are ready to let go. We don't.

How do I clean?

The cleaning is very simple. It's so easy that your intellect has a hard time understanding that by just repeating "I love you" or "Thank you" in your mind, you are actually cleaning. When you say "I love you" or "Thank you" or you use any of the Ho'oponopono tools, you are taking 100% responsibility. You're saying "I am sorry, please forgive me for whatever is in me that has created this."

Why do I have to clean all the time?

Maybe you think nothing is happening. Everything seems ok at the moment. But the cleaning must be done all the time because the memories in the subconscious mind play all the time. Non-stop. Let me give you an example: Think of a CD player. The CD is playing but maybe the volume is down and you can't hear anything. So our memories actually play 24 hours a day, seven days a week and sometimes the volume is down. That's why it's so important to do the cleaning all the time, moment by moment.

By cleaning all the time, you prevent things from coming. You never know how many doors you've closed and how many doors will open, that would never have opened, because of your cleaning.

How do I clean all the time?

Your biological children watch you. They don't listen to you. It's the same with your Inner Child. Once you decide to take 100% responsibility and practice Ho'oponopono instead of jumping around from one spiritual practice to another, your Inner Child or subconscious mind will do it for you. It will happen automatically. Your Inner Child does your breathing, pumps your heart, runs your body. In that same way, your Inner Child can do the cleaning for you automatically. But again, you need to ride one horse. If you practice different things, your Inner Child gets confused and doesn't know what to do when a problem comes up.

What happens when I clean?

The intellect initiates the cleaning. It's the part of us that chooses to clean, to let go instead of engage. Once the intellect decides to take 100% responsibility, something like an order goes to the Inner Child, the subconscious mind or Unihipili as it is called in Hawaiian. The Inner Child is the one that makes the connection to the superconscious, the Aumakua in us. The Aumakua refines the petition. This part of us is perfect and knows what we are ready to let go of. The Aumakua presents our petition directly to Divinity. That's basically how it works. But remember, you don't need to know or understand. You just need to initiate the cleaning. Just do it!

Every time you do the cleaning, something happens even if you don't see it or feel it. TRUST! Remember, no expectations. You don't know where it's going to come from. Be open. Be happy as a child and you will be amazed.

How long does it take to see results from cleaning?

There's no specific answer. Sometimes you'll see the results right away. Other times it can take longer. Remember that people come into your life to give you one more chance. The people you live with, the people you work with, are the ones with whom you have more "stuff" to clean.

You're doing this cleaning to be at peace no matter what's happening. You clean without expecting specific results in a certain length of time. You're going to be at peace even if the other person doesn't change or leave. You can be at peace if you have money or if you don't have money. You want to be at peace no matter what's going on around you. The change will be in God's time, not in your time. But know that it will be perfect timing.

Do I just sit and clean? What about taking action?

You always want to be cleaning, before, during and after taking action. Constant cleaning gives you more opportunities to come from Inspiration. You have to do what feels good in your heart. But even when you take action from Inspiration, you want to keep cleaning moment by moment so you can be open and flexible to doors that might open. Maybe a change of course will be the correct thing to do. You want to be awake and conscious of the opportunities that might present.

How can I clean with my expectations?

Expectations are also memories and are just in the way of getting what is right and perfect for you in an easy way. Let go of expectations. Let go of thinking you know what is right and perfect. When you catch yourself expecting something whether good or bad, let go. Go back to being the innocent child of God that you are. Be open to miracles.

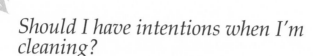

Should I have intentions when I'm cleaning?

Intentions are also memories. You want to clean with intentions. You want to let go and set yourself free. Again, you want to do it God's way, not your way.

Why is my connection with my Inner Child so important?

You can talk to your child any time, when you're driving, when you're waiting in line. It's important that you say "I love you" and "Thank you" as often as you can to this part of you. These are great tools to use with your Inner Child: thank you for doing our breathing, for taking care of our body, for pumping our heart.

If anything is causing you pain or suffering right now, you can ask your child to let go. Work with your child coming from love, not forcing anything, like with affirmations. We love our enemies who are simply the memories stored in our subconscious mind or Inner

Child. We don't resist our enemies. Love can heal anything. Not only does your Inner Child hold all your memories and run your body, it's also the part of you that makes the connection with your Superconscious mind and from your Superconscious to Divinity. Your Inner Child is also the manifestor in your life.

Talk to your child. Mentally think of hugging your child, holding his or her hands. Know that a man can have an Inner Child who is a girl and vice versa, so no expectations. You may see or hear this child when you talk to him/her. Some of you may not have any experience at all and that is ok too. Just do it. Again, no expectations.

When you talk to your child, you're actually cleaning. In other words, the caring of your Inner Child is also a cleaning tool. Maybe you want to think about all the things you would like to let go of, physically and emotionally. So you ask your child with love and compassion: "please let go." Any time is a good time to talk to your Unihipili; maybe you want to say I am sorry for all the lifetimes that I neglected you, that I ignored you. Maybe you want to promise and reassure this child in you that you will not abandon him or her again.

If you are looking for the perfect partner, your Inner Child is it. It is the one you are looking for.

How can I clean automatically?

Teach your Inner Child the cleaning process and be consistent with your Ho'oponopono practice so your child doesn't get confused with other things. This way your child will clean when you neglect to clean. When your child is clear and knows that every time a problem comes up, you are willing to take 100% responsibility and clean, your child will do it for you. You will be on automatic. Your child is doing it for you.

I would like to make something clear, 100% responsibility doesn't mean guilty or that you are a sinner. It means you are responsible for the memories playing inside of yourself.

If you have a tool menu or if you have taken the classes, you can put the tool menu underneath your pillow. The subconscious mind never sleeps, so your subconscious or Inner Child will actually read the tool menu. Now it's even more likely that you'll be cleaning 24 hours a day. It's your intellect that gets tired, not the subconscious mind. Since the subconscious never sleeps, you can clean when your intellect is not there.

If you go to bed worrying, you probably aren't going to clean so I recommend that you fall asleep cleaning by saying "thank you, thank you, thank you, I love you, I love you, I love you." Even if you're mad, anxious, or upset at somebody at least you kind of let go and now you're more likely to clean while you sleep too.

And you'll be surprised how often when you forget to clean, even during the day, you'll have the feeling that your Unihipili, your Inner Child or subconscious, is actually cleaning. In order for this to happen, it's important to train your Inner Child that every time there is a problem, you are 100% responsible and you let go.

Dreams are also memories, opportunities to clean, so it's great to have our child doing the cleaning, even while we sleep!

What if more stuff comes up when I'm cleaning?

You're cleaning and now you notice more things that were there before but you weren't aware of. Now you are clearer. Now you know better. God will give you lots of opportunities to clean because now you know how to clean!

Remember, these things that come up are really blessings, opportunities to grow and find out who you really are. They aren't tests or punishments.

Who am I saying "I'm sorry" to?

You're saying "sorry" to your enemies. Your enemies are your memories, and they are inside of yourself.

Maybe you're saying "sorry" to yourself? Maybe you're saying "sorry" to the Divinity in you?

You'll never know and you don't need to know. You don't need to understand this either. You just have to do it. Once the conscious mind or intellect makes the choice to let go, the process of transmutation will take place. We don't need to know what happens or how it happens. We just need to do it.

Do I need to repeat the whole cleaning sentence?

No, each tool is a cleaning process in itself. The entire phrase: "I'm sorry, please forgive me for whatever is in me that is creating this" is already built in the Ho'oponopono tools. So when you say "I Love you" or "Thank you," you know you are taking 100% responsibility and saying: "I'm sorry, please forgive me for whatever is in me that is creating this."

The tools are like the icon in the monitor on your computer. You just need to double click and you don't need to understand how the program opens.

Through the years the cleaning has become much easier. Please don't take them for granted. It took a lot of cleaning from a lot of people for many years to get where we are today.

If I just say "Thank you," am I cleaning?

Yes, it's just as simple as saying "Thank you." The cleaning wasn't as easy twelve years ago when I took the training. But every tool is sacred, even though they sometimes seem ridiculous or too easy. As Ihaleakalá says, "God doesn't know what else to do to make it easier so that we will do it." And even though the tools are easy, we still don't do the cleaning. Whatever tool you choose, you are simply saying, "I am sorry, please forgive me for whatever is in me that has created this."

When I say "Thank you" or "I love you," do I need to mean it or feel it?

When you delete something on your computer, do you need to smile while you do it? Do you have to mean it? Do you have to feel like deleting? No, of course not. It's the same with Ho'oponopono. Just do it. Press that delete key!

I encourage you to say "Thank you" or "I love you" aloud to people. This will definitely close doors, so that other doors can open. But in Ho'oponopono you can say it mentally and it will work too. Ho'oponopono works for everybody. It doesn't matter if you believe or not or if you mean it or not. When you say "I love you", or "Thank you" in your mind, you are letting go. You're giving permission to Divinity to take care of your problems.

Can I clean for someone else?

You are the problem. If you have somebody suffering in your life, it's your memories, your thoughts of that person suffering. If you really want to help, you let go of whatever is in you that manifests as that person having a problem. You never know what memories you're cleaning with. Whatever comes up, it is up to you to take 100% responsibility and let go.

You are always cleaning for yourself but as you clean for yourself, whatever gets erased from you gets erased from the other person. If you want to help, give your problems and others' to God. He knows better!

Why don't I need to talk to anybody?

Whatever comes off of you comes off of
everybody else. Remember that people come into
your life to give you one more chance. They are
your teachers, a gift in your life even if it doesn't
look that way. Talking doesn't help. Talking is like
resisting. We know that what we resist persists.
When we talk, we attract more memories. We
attract more of what we don't want. If we didn't
talk, we wouldn't have as many problems.

Letting go, keeping our mouths shut and doing
the cleaning, gives us more chances to come
from Inspiration. We might end up saying
exactly what the other person wanted to hear.
Or we might not have to say anything, and
the other person will change or get their own
Inspiration because we clean.

Discussing, having the last word, being right
doesn't work. Again, when we clean, whatever
gets erased from us gets erased from them. The
most amazing things happen when we do this
cleaning. As you change, everything changes
because they were just your memories.

Can I share cleaning with someone else?

Whom are you going to tell? Nobody's out there. You're the problem and you're responsible. We always tend to tell people what to do and give advice. We think we can help somebody else, but again, we're the ones responsible. If you really want to help people, you have to let go so God can do what is right for everybody. God created them and knows what is right and perfect for them. We don't even know what is right for us!

Everything comes back to you, the good and the bad. You don't want to be giving the wrong information or the wrong advice to people. God waits for our permission and doesn't invade our privacy as we do with others. Everybody has free choice.

Which is the right tool to use?

No matter what tools you have, they are all interchangeable. The reason why there are many, is because we all have different tastes.

You should use the one that feels right to you. When a problem comes up, please ask: How do I clean with this? Ihaleakalá says that if you hear something that is ridiculous, you do it, because you heard correctly. God has a great sense of humor.

Can I have my own cleaning tools?

Yes, you can have your own cleaning tools. The more you clean, the more you will be at zero. At zero you receive new information, new ideas, and you will act upon this new information without thinking. When a problem comes up ask "how do I clean?" You might hear or be guided to do something. Do it because you heard correctly. Trust your own Inspiration. You have the answers inside yourself.

What is the difference between Inspiration and Intuition?

Inspiration is new information; new ideas. They come from God/Universe. Like the idea of the

Internet. The person that thought of that doesn't know where he got it from.

Intuition is replayed memories. Our Inner Child (our subconcious mind) could warn us that something that happened before is about to happen again.

Am I doing it right?

Again, no expectations. Do your best. God is just waiting for you to give permission. There is no such thing as a wrong way to do it. Just do it! The most important thing is that you are willing to take responsibility for whatever is in you and you are willing to let go, knowing that you don't know anything.

God (Love) can heal anything. Your job is to give permission. It takes a lot of trust. It's uncertain. It can be scary, but it works every time, even if you cannot feel it, even if you cannot see it. It is the law of the Universe: you knock, the door opens. It works 24 hours a day. It never closes for holidays and it doesn't take siestas. It is waiting for you. And it is free!

What memories are we erasing?

We are not the ones erasing or deciding what we erase, thank God! God or that part of us that knows us better is the one deciding what we are letting go. You might think you are cleaning with a specific person or situation but your memories are connected and like in the spider web, when you pull one everything shakes and moves. The person or situation you think you are cleaning with, is just the trigger point and things are never what you think they are.

What if I don't want to erase a good memory?

What part of you is saying a memory is good? It's the part of you that does the judging and has the opinions, the part of you that doesn't really know anything. Again, you want to be free. You want to be at zero. At zero there is no information, no good or bad, correct or incorrect. At zero you aren't talking or listening either. You're at zero.

You want to set yourself free. It's not about you deciding what to erase and what not to erase. God will always bring you what is perfect and right for you. You don't know what that is. Let go of the good and let go of the bad. Set yourself free.

Can I pray directly to God?

The intellect cannot communicate directly with God. The petition goes from the mother (conscious/intellect), downward to the child (subconscious), then up to the father (superconscious), and finally up to Divinity. The intellect doesn't have a clue about God, has never seen God. Remember, the Inner Child is the one making that connection to God.

Cleaning is a way of asking, a way of giving permission to God to bring you what is right and perfect. No matter how you do it, even if you think you're talking directly to God, you are always going through your Inner Child. Your Inner Child is the one making that connection. You can ask your Inner Child to let go and let God. Your child understands.

Why should I love my pain? Or love having cancer?

What we resist persists. Pain sometimes can be something positive. You might be letting go of memories through pain. The body is memories. When we do the cleaning, we do it to be at peace with the pain, at peace with the cancer. We do not do it for the pain to go away—that's expectations. Love can heal anything. Yes, say "I love you" to the cancer. It's a way of letting go. Many times people ask why couldn't God take it all at once. We could say, "Ok, I accept, I am 100% responsible, please take them all"! Ihaleakalá explained to me, that the body is also memories, and our bodies couldn't resist it, we would turn like prunes if God would take all our memories at once. The beautiful thing is that God knows what we are ready to let go, what we are ready to heal.

What about planning and setting goals?

Do you want to tell God what is right for you and when He should bring it to you? God is not your concierge. Even if you continue planning and setting goals, do yourself a favor and let go. Be open to other roads, other doors that might open on the way. You don't want to miss them.

What about affirmations?

Affirmations are treating God as a servant, giving instructions to God because you think you know what is right and perfect. With Ho'oponopono and the cleaning, you are giving permission to God who knows better to bring you whatever is right and perfect. You don't want to be in the way or telling God what to do. Affirmations are also forcing the Inner Child. When he/she hears you repeat "I am happy, I am happy," the child knows it's a lie.

What about visualizations?

Visualizations are also "orders" to God. He is the one creating when you use any of the tools. If you can see God's work, if you can see God's creation and transmutation, good for you. But you are not the one doing it. Your job is just to say it or just to do it and then God is the one who creates. God is the one who will do whatever is perfect and right for you, but He doesn't need you giving him directions of what colors to use, or how to do it, or what the results should be. Again, affirmations and visualizations are giving directions to God.

For example, when you clean using the Thank You tool (just repeating thank you, thank you, thank you in your mind), God might do something different every time you say it because God knows what is right and perfect for you at that moment. You just need to say it, not visualize it. Let God do His work.

What is the purpose of existence?

We are here to make amends, to let go of whatever is not us, and to discover who we really are. So as we let go, as we erase memories, we re-discover ourselves, who we really are. We are not here to make money or to have a relationship. We are here to clean and be ourselves. When you are yourself, everything else comes.

Are Huna and Ho'oponopono the same thing?

Not really. Huna was created and invented by men. Ho'oponopono comes from other galaxies. Huna comes more from forcing the child (subconscious) to attract to us what we think is right for us. Ho'oponopono comes more from Love.

Is Ho'oponopono the same as The Secret?

With The Secret, we tell God what we want. We give orders to God. The Secret also assumes we are aware of all our thoughts and that we know what is right and perfect for us.

In Ho'oponopono, we let God direct us. We don't tell Him what to do, we allow Him to guide us. Ho'oponopono tells us that only God knows what is right and perfect for us.

It's important to realize you're aware of only 15 bits of information per second. You actually have 11,000,000 bits of information per second that you're not aware of, like the CDs playing in the CD player with the volume down (remember the example above?). When you do affirmations, you're just manipulating the 15 bits you're conscious of while the 11,000,000 are playing in the background! Ho'oponopono works on the 11,000,000 and does it effortlessly.

Well, I hope you have enjoyed this reading. Remember that you need to remind yourself to stay conscious and do Ho'oponopono cleaning all the time. You need to unlearn and relearn, so I hope you read this book again and again, knowing that every time you read it, you will find something new, because you are anew moment by moment. As you practice, practice and practice, without expectations, you will experience the magic, see the results, be happier, find peace, and set yourself free!!

God Bless You.

Credits

THE FOUNDATION OF I, INC. (Freedom Of the Cosmos). Volcano, Hawaii. Tools, material and information used with permission, about the Hawaiian art of Ho'oponopono given through the seminars: *Self-Identity through Ho'oponopono* • *www.hooponopono.org*

Excerpts from *Way of the Peaceful Warrior,* by Dan Millman New Revised Edition © 2000. Used with permission from New World Library, Novato, CA 94949 • *www.newworldlibrary.com*

Excerpts from *The Power of Now,* by Eckhart Tolle © 1999. Used with permission from New World Library, Novato, CA 94949 • *www.newworldlibrary.com*

The Teaching of Buddha. Tokio: Bukkyo Dendo Kyokai, 1966

The Indigo Children. References of James Twyman communications with the Children • *www.emmisaryoflove.com*

About the Author

Mabel Katz not only inspires change, SHE will change your life forever!

Mabel Katz instills inspiration that will last a lifetime. With her inspirational approach, Mabel gives people the tools they need to change their lives and create lasting results. Her approach goes to people's core, their soul. Many have said she's changed their lives forever.

Born in Argentina, Mabel moved to Los Angeles in 1983 where she became a successful accountant, business consultant and tax advisor. In 1997 Mabel started her own company, *Your Business, Inc.*, a step that not only enhanced her own success but also increased her ability to work more directly with others. Her company had prospered by helping new and established businesses expand and grow.

Mabel is internationally acclaimed as a foremost authority on the ancient Hawaiian art of problem solving called **Ho'oponopono**. The essence of this art is simple: You can be at peace no matter what is going on around you. For twelve years Mabel studied intensively with the Master Ihaleakalá Hew Len, Ph.D.

Mabel is the Author of **The Easiest Way**, *Solve your problems and take the road to love, happiness, wealth and the life of your dreams.* The latest release, is a Special Edition of the book that includes a special bonus, **The Easiest Way to Understanding Ho'oponopono**, The *Clearest Answers to Your Most Frequently Asked Questions.* This Special Edition answers the how, what, when and where, of this ancient art. How to clean and erase our programs and get back to Zero. Mabel is also a contributing author to, **Inspiration to Realization, Thank God I** … and **Más Allá del Psicoanálisis** *(Beyond the Psychoanalysis).*

Mabel's newest book, **The Easiest Way to Live**, *Let go of the past, live in the present and change your life forever*, deals concisely with issues such as; the intellect, letting go, memories, forgiveness, expectations, judgments, emotions, addictions, happiness, success and money. This book is the most organized interpretation for living the easiest way through the art of Ho'oponopono. It takes you to a whole new level of understanding; how to let go of the past, live in the present and open yourself to all the opportunities of the future.

Mabel's trainings have been attracting more parents to bring their children to learn the art of Ho'oponopono. This has delighted Mabel as she loves working with children. It also made her realize that there was no age appropriate literature on the subject and that she wanted to share with children the messages she would have liked to know as a child. Mabel is now elated to announce her first children's book, **The Easiest Way to Grow**, *Messages You Will Be Glad to Know*, a book filled with beautiful illustrations and words that offer the basic messages of Ho'oponopono in a very inspiring manner for children ages 3 to 100.

Zero Frequency®, *Maximum results, minimum effort*, is the book she is currently writing. This book was inspired by her realization that no matter what is going on around you if you are at zero, (no judgments, no opinions, no expectations, or beliefs) you are open and allowing that the flow of life puts you at the right time at the right place.

With her unmistakable style and grace, Mabel transcends languages. Her books have been translated and published into English, Spanish, Korean, Portuguese, Swedish, German, French, Russian, Chinese, Hebrew, Romanian, Italian, Czech, Japanese, Croatian, Polish and Hungarian.

A star in LA's Latino community, Mabel hosted the popular radio and television program, called **Despertar** *(Awakening),* and the **Mabel Katz Show** where she empowered Latino's by giving them the tools to start or grow a business, have fulfilled relationships and find financial success.

As a result of her personal and business accomplishments and her generosity of spirit, Mabel has received acclaim on the local and national levels. Some of her national recognition includes; *Business Woman of the Year For 2005* by the *LA Metropolitan Chamber of Commerce.* In 2006 she received the *Sol Azteca Award* and the prestigious *Latin Business Association's Members Choice Award.* Also in 2006 she was one of only nine women nationwide to receive the coveted *Anna Maria Arias Memorial Business Fund Award.*

Mabel is now acclaimed at the international level. Ten years after starting her own business, Mabel decided to give up her successful accounting firm and talk show aspirations to accept the invitations she receives from all over the world. She is now on a journey that is taking her around the world as an author, seminar leader and speaker, inspiring many different cultures and languages with her simple and yet very effective and profound message.

Mabel is available for interviews, speaking engagements and seminars.

...

Telephone/Fax: (818) 668-2085 | *support@mabelkatz.com*

www.mabelkatz.com | *www.innerpeaceISworldpeace.com*
www.hooponoponoway.com | *www.thezerofrequencymethod.com*

Peace and Ho'oponopono Resources from Mabel Katz

The Sacred Ho'oponopono Membership

www.HooponoponoWay.com/memberships

As a Sacred Ho'oponopono Member you get weekly Ho'oponopono audios and inspirations and the daily community reminders to stay present and let go moment by moment! Daily Ho'oponopono community support has proven to keep members on track with the cleaning, specially when going through challenging times regarding health, loneliness, money and relationships.

World Peace Campaign - Peace Begins with ME

www.peacewithinISworldpeace.com

"Peace within IS world peace" is the theme that will connect people all over the world who will stand up for peace and affirm "Peace Begins with Me!" The message is clear: It is time to unite on a global level to create inner peace to spread world peace. Take action and join us. Together we can make a difference. Make sure you join the Peace Newsletter and learn how you can help to spread World Peace!
www.peacewithinISworldpeace.com/free-widget

Imagine... Rebuilding Your Life In 40 Days & 40 Nights...

www.MabelKatz.com/hooponopono-40-days-40-nights.html

Mabel takes you on a wonderful journey...A Journey of inspiration that will support you and help you find your way "Out of the Desert" into "The Fertile Lands" of all possibilities...By investing 10 minutes per morning, and 10 minutes per evening you will improve 40 areas of your life. Do you deserve to invest $1.00 per day in yourself?

Free Resources in English about Ho'oponopono

www.MabelKatz.com/resources-events-hooponopono.htm

Information about Mabel, calendar, audios, videos and unique resources.

Mabel's Blog, Forum, News and WOW Histories

www.HooponoponoWay.net/blog/

Read Mabel's latest Ho'oponopono blog posts, articles, and more. Share your story about Ho'oponopono and leave a comment.

Zero Frequency® Mabel Katz
Maximum Results with Minimum Effort

www.TheZeroFrequencyMethod.com

Zero Frequency® is the Perfect frequency, no static or bad connections. No memories, no programming, no judgments, no opinions, no struggles, no fears, just pure inspiration. At Zero you discover your true identity, knowing your true identity is the key to finding your paradise.

Follow Mabel on Twitter

www.twitter.com/MabelKatz
Read Mabel's latest Tweets on her Ho'oponopono journey.

Follow Mabel on Facebook

www.facebook.com/MabelKatzFanPage
Interact with Mabel on her Facebook page.

Follow Mabel on Youtube

www.youtube.com/MabelKatz
Videos & Interviews with Mabel on her Youtube page.

Leave a voice/text testimonial:

512-827-0505, ext. 9450 or *support@mabelkatz.com*
Leave a voice/text testimonial (512) 827-0505 ext 6563 or support@mabelkatz.com Mabel would love to hear your testimonial on how the Peace campaign and Ho'oponopono have touched your life.

How to Engage the Author

Mabel Katz is an internationally acclaimed speaker, author, and seminar leader who is recognized as a leading authority on Ho'oponopono, an ancient Hawaiian art and practice for achieving greater clarity of purpose and living and working more effectively. She has crafted a series of keynotes, talks, and seminars for corporations, businesses, and individuals – including seminars for children – that apply the practices of Ho'oponopono to bring companies closer to their full potential and give people an edge at work and in all areas of life.

Based on using forgiveness and gratitude, her presentations focus on practical ways for reaching what she calls Zero Frequency®, a state where we are free of restrictive memories and limiting self-talk. From the clarity of Zero, outstanding solutions become apparent and excellent choices can be made.

Mabel is also rapidly gaining acclaim for her work in support of world peace. She has spoken in front of national senates and other influential government bodies and has presented at the United Nations. She has addressed multi-cultural audiences, including those of diverse ethnicities in the Middle East.

Mabel is available for keynotes, talks and seminars for executives, managers, employees, individuals and children.

For more information on Mabel's workshops, seminars, speaking engagements or book orders you can contact the author at:

Your Business, Inc.
P.O. Box 427
Woodland Hills, CA 91365

Telephone/Fax: (818) 668-2085
support@mabelkatz.com
www.MabelKatz.com
www.HooponoponoWay.com
www.theZeroFrequencyMethod.com
www.peacewithinISworldpeace.com

The Easiest Way

Solve your problems and take the road to love, happiness, wealth and the life of your dreams.

Table of Contents

The Easiest Way
to Understanding Ho'oponopono
The Clearest Answers to Your Most Frequently Asked Questions

Table of Contents